Momma Would You Ever?

written by
Rebecca Marklund

illustrated by
Veronika Hipolito

Momma Would You Ever?
Copyright © 2023 by Rebecca Marklund

Tellwell Talent
www.tellwell.ca

ISBN
978-0-2288-7041-8 (Hardcover)
978-0-2288-7040-1 (Paperback)
978-0-2288-7042-5 (eBook)

This book is dedicated to:

my sons, my life, my loves, my inspiration
for being brave enough to ask such questions

and

to those who have wrestled and chosen well
between
the best, the good, and the better

One day, a gentle little boy took
his momma's hand and asked...

"Momma, would you ever trade me
for all the gold in the world?"

"Never," she replied, and she hugged him close.

The next week, the growing boy came to her again.

"Momma, would you ever trade me for all the diamonds in the world?"

"Never," she replied, and
she hugged him close.

The next month, the eager boy
came to his momma again.

"Momma, would you ever trade me
for all the books in the world?"

"Never," she replied, and
she hugged him close.

The next year, the adventurous boy came to his momma again.

"Momma, would you ever trade me
for all the trips in the world?"

"Never," she replied, and she hugged him close.

After a few years had passed, the lanky teen boy came to his momma again.

"Momma, would you ever trade me for all the land and houses in the world?"

"Never," she replied, and
she hugged him close.

Time passed, and the boy grew
into a fine young man.

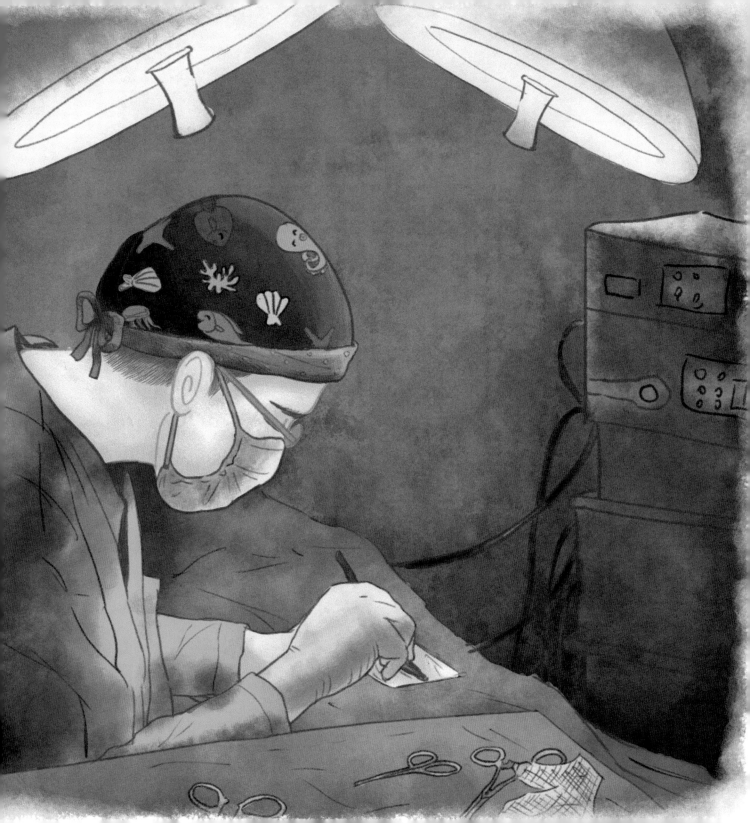

The momma grew into a
fine old momma.

The man came to his momma.

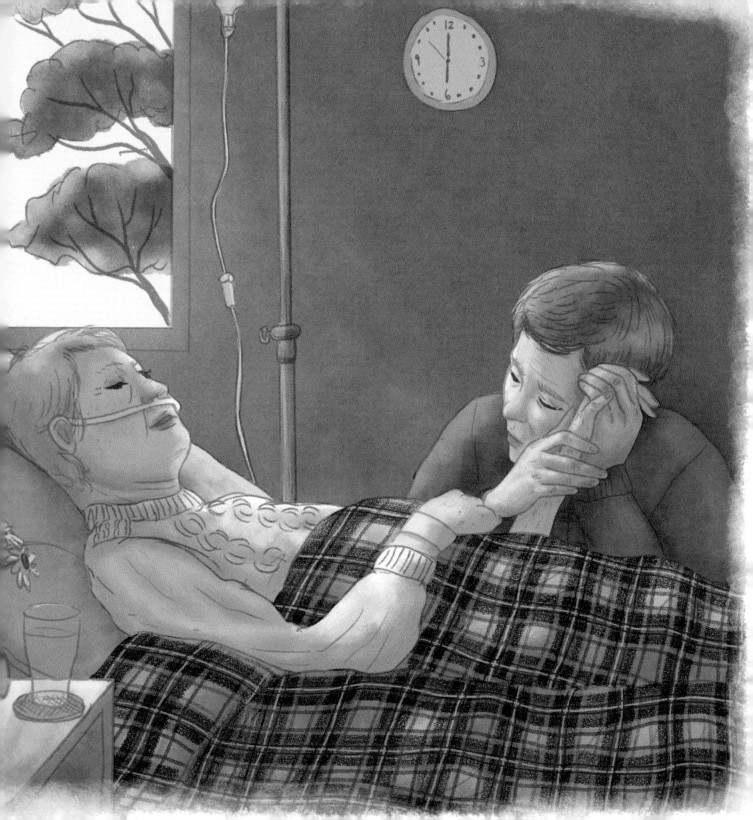

"Momma, would you ever trade me
for all the time in the world?"

"Never," she replied, and
he hugged her close.

"Dad, would you ever trade me
for all the gold in the world?"

"Never," he said, and they walked on.

Rebecca lives on the beautiful west coast of British Columbia with her four sons. She is a homeschool educator, a nurse, and an author, with a passion for spending quality time with her children and exploring the natural beauty of the surrounding forests and oceans. Rebecca is dedicated to learning and experiencing life with her family, as well as actively participating in and contributing to her local community. Her interests include family, education, botany, and promoting health and wellness for women and children.

Manufactured by Amazon.ca
Bolton, ON

33620160R00033